THE AUTHOR

GEORGIA HARKNESS, professor of applied theology at the Pacific School of Religion, Berkeley, California, was selected in 1952 by *The Christian Century* as one of the six most influential church women in the United States.

An ordained Methodist minister, Dr. Harkness has attended most of the major ecumenical conferences in both this country and abroad in recent years. Among these were the Lund Conference on Faith and Order, to which she served as a Methodist delegate; and the Evanston Assembly of the World Council of Churches, where she was consultant.

Prior to accepting her present position in 1950, Dr. Harkness taught at Garrett Biblical Institute in Evanston, and earlier, served on the faculties of Elmira and Mount Holyoke colleges.

A native of New York State, Georgia Harkness attended Cornell University, and took graduate work at Boston University, Harvard, Yale Divinity School, and Union Theological Seminary. Widely known as a writer, she was co-winner of the Abingdon Award in 1948 with her *Prayer and the Common Life*.

THE GOSPEL AND OUR WORLD

BOOKS BY THE SAME AUTHOR

PRAYER AND THE COMMON LIFE

UNDERSTANDING THE CHRISTIAN FAITH

THE DARK NIGHT OF THE SOUL

THE GLORY OF GOD

THE FAITH BY WHICH THE CHURCH LIVES

RELIGIOUS LIVING

THE RECOVERY OF IDEALS

THE RESOURCES OF RELIGION

HOLY FLAME

JOHN CALVIN: THE MAN AND HIS ETHICS

CONFLICTS IN RELIGIOUS THOUGHT

THE CHURCH AND THE IMMIGRANT

The Gospel and Our World

by

GEORGIA HARKNESS

1966

ABINGDON PRESS
NEW YORK • NASHVILLE

THE GOSPEL AND OUR WORLD

Library of Congress Catalog Card Number: 49-11676

C

SET UP, PRINTED, AND BOUND BY THE PARTHENON PRESS, AT NASHVILLE, TENNESSEE, UNITED STATES OF AMERICA

Acknowledgments

THIS BOOK has grown out of three addresses prepared for the E. T. Earl Lectureship. To the Pacific School of Religion, under whose auspices the Earl Lectures are given, I am indebted both for the invitation to give them and for many courtesies on the occasion of their delivery in Berkeley during February 22-24, 1949, at the Interdenominational Pastoral Conference. To the president of the school, Dr. Ronald Bridges, I owe a particular debt.

A portion of chapter five was first written for the Interseminary Conference at Miami University in June, 1947, and later printed in the *Christian Century* under the title "The Layman's World." With some alterations it is reprinted here by permission of that journal.

To my friend and housemate Verna Miller, who typed the manuscript and gave me counsel and encouragement in its preparation, my gratitude as always is great.

Contents

Introduction

THE THESIS of this book is a fairly simple one. It is that the churches of America, though far from decadent, are doing much less effective work than they might be doing with their resources, and that the major cause of the difficulty lies in failure to present the meaning and claims of the Christian faith in terms that seem vital to the common man. In short, there is need of a much closer connection than we have had thus far between theology and evangelism.

The Christian faith is both something to be believed and something to be lived. The gospel comes to us in two modes, as suggested by the dual meaning of the term "faith." Our faith is all that inherited body of Christian belief, requiring constant re-examination and reinterpretation, which gives us assured convictions regarding God and his relations to the world. Our faith is also what Paul declared it to be, "the power of God unto salvation to every one that believeth." These two meanings of faith are intimately related but not identical, and the relations between them are seldom sharply defined.

Concern with the gospel in one of these senses does

not guarantee its presence in the other. In dealing as theologians with the Christian faith as a body of truth, we have often been too abstract, too limited in our diction to traditional terminology, possibly too afraid to be simple lest our peers might suspect our lack of theological acumen! In proclaiming the gospel as evangelists we have been concerned to make a point of contact with the people, but because the faith as thus presented has been set in too narrow a context and has not been addressed to the mind as well as the heart, it has often failed to lead to a permanent and constructive reorientation of life. In our sermonizing we have sometimes made an effective synthesis but unfortunately have often fallen midway between the two, failing either to clarify Christian belief for the people in the pews or to open the channels to God's saving power.

In the first chapter we shall rapidly survey the assets and liabilities of the American churches. To keep the focus on the American scene is not to disregard the importance of the world church. In many respects what can be said of church life in America can be said of the world. Yet in other respects—notably our ecclesiastical diversity, the freedom of the Church from state control, and the predominance of liberalism and fundamentalism rather than the new orthodoxy as the prevailing theological climate—our situation is different, and it will sharpen the discussion to keep it within such bounds. We shall then look at the state of mind of the modern man in the American scene and try to outline what the Christian gospel has to offer him by way of something to believe and something to live by.

In the third and fourth chapters we shall examine what a closer synthesis of theology with evangelism might mean in personal religious living. It may not be out of order here to make some comparisons as to the effectiveness in this field of three dominant types of American church life—the Roman Catholic, the fundamentalist Protestant, and the liberal—mainly with a view to seeing what can be learned from types other than our own. However, the deeper purpose of this section will be to look at the bearing of Christian faith both as truth and as power, regardless of denominational or ecclesiastical affiliations, on man's perennial problems of frustration and fear, unmerited suffering, sin and death.

In the final section we must look outward to the social scene. Men everywhere are trying desperately to save the world from another war, from economic catastrophe, from one form or another of social disease that threatens the death of civilization. We preachers and professors do our share of talking on this score. Laymen, who as a rule live closer to the political and economic struggle, often listen politely but regard our views as suspect. If the social gospel were more firmly grounded in the basic and ultimate truths of Christianity, it might carry more practical weight. In any case, our inquiry at this point must ask what sort of "theology for the social gospel" will square with the eternal truths of the Christian faith and thus be adequate to throw light on the decisions required of our time.

A word may be in order as to the general viewpoint. I speak as an evangelical liberal, perhaps as a "middle-of-the-roader" in theology, but certainly as one who believes that the truth is seldom found in extremes. Central truths can be revolutionary if put to work. Such central Christian truth is found best, not through one channel only, but through a synthesis of the findings of philosophy, theology, the Bible, and Christian experience, guided throughout by what God has shown us of himself in the mind of Christ.

For longer than I can remember my life has been interwoven with the Church, and during the past ten years I have been brought closer to it both through seminary teaching and through contacts in the ecumenical movement. Since I believe profoundly that the Church with all its faults has a gospel of truth and power which—if its truth and power are united and released to the people—can save the world, I invite you to examine with me this gospel and search for a way out of our present evil days.

CHAPTER I

Disease and Diagnosis

THE STATE of the American churches today is neither good nor bad, but indifferent. Taken as a whole, they are not sick or well, but in that uncomfortable in-between stage at which the patient is well enough to keep going and at least perfunctorily do his work, yet unable to do it with zest, enthusiasm, and effectiveness. The Body of Christ has many members, and not all of them are diseased. The creaking of rheumatic ecclesiastical joints does not necessarily mean that sight and hearing are impaired, and myopia on the race question and kindred matters does not mean that all the arteries are hardened. It is clear that we have all sinned and fallen short of the glory of God, but it can hardly be said in a diagnostic sense that there is no health in us. Yet we are so far from full health, and hence so far from glorifying God as we ought, that the situation is serious. If any remedy is to be found, it must straightway be discovered and acted upon for the good of the patient and still more for his effective service to God in a world that desperately needs what the Church has to offer.

In the search for the roots of the present malaise of the churches a canvass of possible causes reveals symptoms of disease, but also highly encouraging evidences of residual health. Does the trouble lie in the lack of membership? Though every church could take care of more members and ought to be receiving more—would be receiving more if a revival of John Wesley or Jonathan Edwards proportions were to sweep the country—the situation at the point of membership is far from unhealthy. According to the latest figures available in the compilation made by the *Christian Herald* and presented in the *Federal Council Information Service* of November 20, 1948, the membership of 253 religious bodies in the United States is now over 77,500,000.[1] This includes 44,571,486 Protestants in 50 churches having a membership of 50,000 or more, with approximately another 1,500,000 in 173 smaller Pentecostal sects, 25,268,173 Roman Catholics, 4,641,000 Jews, nearly 1,000,000 Eastern Orthodox, 70,000 Buddhists, and 150,000 members of the International General Assembly of Spiritualists. The most significant deductions from these figures are, first, that more than half of the people of the United States are now members of religious bodies—in the neighborhood of 53 per cent—and second, that growth in church membership reveals a steady increase,

[1] The number given is 77,386,188. However, this does not include the membership of the Church of Christ, Scientist, since this body's *Church Manual* forbids the numbering of people and the reporting of such statistics for publication.

not only numerically but in proportion to the general population. A survey of membership trends from 1926 to 1947 shows that church membership increased about 40 per cent in that period, while the population of the country as a whole increased only 24 per cent. Compared with the approximately 5 per cent who were members of churches at the end of the colonial period our present situation is not bad,[2] and with more than half the population in churches Christians could make a very significant impact on our society if these churches were acting vitally and concertedly.

Or does the trouble lie in our unholy divisions, of which we have been hearing much in these days of new ecumenical emphasis? Certainly this is a symptom of grave disorder, for these same statistics point to the existence of 223 different Protestant bodies in the United States, only 50 of which have memberships of 50,000 or more. Most of these have names quite unfamiliar to —in many instances never heard of by—the membership of the larger bodies. Ask an ordinary Baptist, whether Northern or Southern, to give the distinguishing characteristics of Duck River Baptists or Two-Seed-in-the-Spirit Predestinarian Baptists or General Six-Principle Baptists or any of the rest of the twenty-three divisions of that communion, and he may hem and haw a little or use his traditional independency flatly to repudiate such nonsense! Many Methodists know that

[2] *Year Book of American Churches,* 1947 ed., p. 159.

The Methodist Church was formed by the union of the Methodist Episcopal Church, the Methodist Episcopal Church, South, and the Methodist Protestant Church; some know that there are also A.M.E. and A.M.E. Zion and C. M. E. churches; relatively few know that in spite of the historic union in 1939 there are still nineteen brands of Methodism in the United States.

Such pluralism in the American ecclesiastical scene is a symptom of disorder. Yet it may be doubted that it is more than a symptom, for the root lies deeper. Indeed, such diversity could be an asset as a demonstration not only of the American way of freedom of worship but of the rich variety of gifts within the household of faith, if the churches understood each other and were working toward a common end.

That there is not now adequate understanding and co-operation is a fact to be admitted and deplored. Yet if one surveys the contemporary scene in perspective, there are important signs of health. The Federal Council of Churches has just finished forty years of significant leadership in co-operative action among the major denominations; there are now more than seven hundred state, county, and city councils of churches across the nation; there is a vast deal of co-operative planning in missions, religious education, relief and reconstruction, stewardship, chaplaincies, women's work, and other agencies of the Church—enough so that the *Plan Book of American Cooperative Christianity*[3] requires nearly a hundred pages to outline the projects of seven great interdenominational organizations along thirty-six different lines. Ecumenicity—before, during, and since Amsterdam—is in the air. The churches not only of the world but of the United States are closer together now than they have ever been in their history. What ails our churches is not basically our divisions but apparently something more malignant, the removal of which could go far toward healing these divisions.

Or is the trouble to be found in lack of financial support? There is clearly a correlation between what people think important and what they are willing to spend money on, and the notoriously low salaries of ministers in comparison with those in other skilled professions may be an index of ill health. Yet the giving of church members in the twenty-six larger denominations reporting to the United Stewardship Council runs in the aggregate well beyond $600,000,000 annually and is increasing steadily. In recent years church people have given with striking generosity to projects for overseas relief, and the salaries of ministers and the local staff are less inadequate than formerly. Clearly, if money could buy health, plenty of churches have enough to purchase it. Yet among the many "weak" churches of the land it is apparent that weakness is not to be precisely cor-

[3] Published for the Inter-Council Field Department by the Friendship Press, New York.

related with the size of the budget. Neither a man's nor a church's life seems to consist primarily in the abundance of the things possessed.

This reference to compensation of the clergy sends us investigating another possible explanation of the Church's mediocre influence in our time. Does it lie in the mediocre quality of its leadership? Certainly without adequate leadership any church is doomed, and this lies close to the heart of the matter. Unless a minister has sufficient training, deep religious experience, good common sense, and a healthy mental attitude toward people and toward his work, he is not likely to make much of a go of his job. And plenty of factors present obstacles. In addition frequently to having personal financial worries, he is expected to be a superman—a brilliant and engaging preacher, an administrator, financier, educator, counselor, pastor, priest, prophet, recreation leader, and general handy man—and when he cannot measure up and criticism begins to be bandied about, he gets discouraged and frustrated. It is not good for any man to receive as many compliments to his face, as many barbs behind his back, as a minister usually gets. Endless meetings, whether called by himself or the denominational overhead, eat into his time for study and leave little time for thinking or for sermon preparation. A thousand details—sometimes important to the lives of people, often trivial—consume his energy. He works too hard and nerve strain wears him out, or he works too little and after a while lethargy turns into laziness. The temptations which assail the spirit of a minister are subtle but powerful, and few fully resist them.

Yet, surprisingly, the churches are full of competent, dedicated, mentally healthy, genuinely able ministers. Not all are such, but the number is very great. At least among the major denominations the leadership of the churches is generally in the hands of persons not only of insight and faith, but of high educational attainments. The number of those who have had both college and seminary training is large and continually rising. There are other professions in which the external educational requirements are higher, but there is no profession in which the combination of training plus the qualities of character essential to leadership is so often high. If the churches are sick, and many ministers along with them, this again is a symptom of a deeper disorder instead of being the fundamental cause.

Or does the trouble lie with the laity? Not only numerically, but from the standpoint of what the world sees of the Church, the laymen make up the greater part of it. If "the Church" is backward in demonstrations of racial equality, or conservative in economics, or lethargic in attacking the causes of war, it is mainly because church members in their actions lag behind the official pronouncements of the Church. There are plenty of such excellent statements—formulated largely by ministers and adopted by the denominations, the Federal Council, and the World Council of Churches—to which we have as yet only faint approximations in the political and social life of the rank and file of church members. Yet when one looks at the individual lives of the laymen in our churches, they are good, bad, and indifferent—with overt badness very much in the minority. In the main they are good, kind, honest people; and in the sins which they recognize to be sins—such as theft, drunkenness, and adultery—the record of church people is generally so good that any aberration is immediately spotted by the press as headline news. In my observation laymen as they come are not nearly so crude or selfishly calculating as they are portrayed in the current best sellers, *The Bishop's Mantle* and *No Trumpet Before Him.* Furthermore, when ministers get discouraged and seem to be accomplishing nothing, again and again their hearts are warmed by the fidelity of those laymen—perhaps only one or two in a congregation—who can always be depended on, who see at least partially what the minister is driving at, who in an unpretentious way are genuine Christian saints. In almost every church there is a "saving remnant," and advance toward the Kingdom seems to come most often through the faithful effort of minorities.

Another aspect of this question is of special relevance to a university community. This is the great dearth of college-trained men and women who work actively in the churches. The very persons who could give most intelligent and virile lay leadership have in many instances either forsaken the Church or are only casually connected with it.

For this there are many reasons, both ideological and social. Bad theology is often heard in churches, and to one steeped in naturalistic presuppositions any theology is apt to be suspect. Worship, to one who does not accept its bases in belief, is apt to seem more like a cultic practice nurtured in mythology than a life-renewing force. Moral injunctions are likely to sound platitudinous and superfluous. During the college years a student's religion must fight its way against the high-pressured tempo of the modern campus, the welter of competing social claims, the campus gods of football or fraternity or romance that leave little time or energy to think about religion and the Church. Then when one graduates it is hard to make the connection. Life is still high-pressured and is again set up around competing domestic or business or social claims. As a result college people often chide the Church for being back-numbered or irrelevant or dull, while in its sickness they who could be its best physicians pass by on the other side and leave it to get sicker.

Yet the situation is not all black. Among faculty members, alumni, and students there are those who do go to church, and a smaller but very precious group of those who work actively in its concerns. Religion is so deep-seated a human interest that it can be snowed under but never completely stifled, and on every campus there is a nucleus of students—sometimes a good many, sometimes a small minority—who care about their faith. Not all of those who are interested in *religion* are interested in the *Church,* but some are; and since the war there has been a decided upturn in the number of those considering the ministry and other forms of Christian service. As compared with twenty years ago when religious interest was more largely funneled through nondenominational agencies, the churches are more active in making contacts with students and among a virile minority are securing a better response. With students as confused and torn with strains as most of them now are, the field is open for an interpretation of Christian faith that will be, as the title of Rufus Jones's last book puts it, "a call to what is vital."

This brings us to the heart of the problem. What are the churches trying to say? Has the Church a message with which really to confront the world? Does the layman or the student hear in the churches what can "speak to his condition"? Does the Christian gospel have in it that which can arrest and alter life? In short, has the gospel any power?

To suggest that it may be the gospel which is at fault is to call in question the foundations on which the Church rests and to which it owes its being. If the

Church has nothing to say that challenges, remakes, upbuilds human life, it is only a respectable and semi-decadent human institution, and nothing to worry much about if it goes out of business. Furthermore, to impugn the power of the gospel to transform life is to defy twenty centuries of Christian history in which it has been doing exactly that. However nerveless it may now seem, Christianity has been the dominant force of the Western world. To imply that there is something wrong with its gospel is but a short step from blasphemy on the one hand and a revelation of ignorance on the other.

Yet the *gospel* and the *communication of the gospel* are two different matters. Its communication is the most important task, under God, that any person can undertake. Upon its appropriation hang the issues of life and death—certainly spiritual life and death, and in the atomic age physical life and death as well—for countless millions of individuals in our time. Yet its communication is on the whole so inadequate that the greater part of our society, whether within or outside of the churches, fail to get any real awareness of the gospel's meaning or its power.

Life goes on, for the most part, in our secular world as if the churches did not exist. The message which the churches attempt to communicate falls on deaf ears, not because the ears are really deaf, but because the Word of God is spoken in so strange a language or in such trivialities that *it fails to be the Word of God* to those who otherwise might hear it. If it is not understood, it is no word at all; if it consists only of moral platitudes or echoes the voice of the secular public, it is no word from God. Into both these pitfalls we have fallen, and unless we straightway by the help of God climb out of them, the Church bids fair to remain in its present enfeebled and impotent state.

On the highest authority we are told, "He that hath ears to hear, let him hear." This is our mandate from Christ—to say what comes to us from God in ways that can be heard. Not all will hear and heed us; not all heard and heeded Jesus. But if the gospel is really proclaimed in ways that reach the mind and heart, it has within it such compelling force that some will listen, some lives will be changed, some changes in society will certainly take place. If it is not proclaimed, or if it is spoken in tones that cannot be heard, no power from God or man will give it saving help.

What then ails our churches? Inadequate numbers, unhealthy divisions, meager financial support, unprophetic leadership, lethargic congregations—all these and many more symptoms of ill health are found. But at the root of them all lies the fact that the very thing for which the Church exists—the proclamation of the gospel—is being in our time so feebly done.

If this primary task were now being effectively accomplished, the churches in carrying a message of healing to a sick world would find healing for themselves. There is no better corrective for a feeling of general malaise than a sense of accomplishment. But as it is, great numbers of our churches drag along, well enough to do a good many things fairly well, not dead or even as near to dying as the cynics are prone to say, yet still not well enough to live, grow, and do their work with effectiveness and power. This sickly state is not a comfortable one. They had better get well soon, or they will soon get worse.

CHAPTER II

What Has the Church to Say?

IN THE PRECEDING chapter attention was focused on the current malaise of the churches. A number of things were found to be wrong, though with hopeful signs of latent health at each point of disorder. The most deep-seated cause of the present malady was found to be in the failure to proclaim the gospel in a way that makes any very significant impact on our world.

The term "Christian gospel," like its correlative term "Christian faith," has two related but not identical meanings. In its initial and basic meaning it signifies "good news," something that quickens the heart, something one rejoices to hear and to tell again. In a derivative sense it means the whole great body of Christian truth which gives validity as well as vitality to what is heard and told. In the first sense the gospel is the Christian evangel; in the second it is Christian belief, which when systematized we call theology. In either use of the term the gospel means the good news spoken by God to us in Christ; but in the first meaning the appeal is to the will for the commitment of life, in the second to the mind for the understanding of truth.

It has been a common and very serious error either to merge or to separate too radically these two meanings of the gospel. The fundamentalists have often assumed that the preaching of "gospel" sermons and the singing of "gospel" hymns, looking toward the winning of converts and witnessing to the glories of the Christian life, made theology unnecessary. This same emphasis, however, has often been joined to a rigidly authoritarian theology which held as suspect the Christian experience of those having a different structure of belief. The liberals have been more conscious of the need of applying human intelligence to the quest for the truth of the gospel, and chastened by an awareness of the fallibility of the human mind, they have been less dogmatic in asserting that God has given to them the full and final disclosure of Christian truth. But this tentativeness regarding our knowledge has had the unfortunate effect in many instances of undercutting the assurance with which the Christian evangel is proclaimed. Thus one group of Christians in propagating the gospel as evangel has propagated with it a theology which cannot stand up under scrutiny, while another group—not always, but too often—has lost the power of the evangel without which there is no true gospel. Whichever way we move, the result seems to be unfortunate.

This situation must be overcome if the churches are to proclaim a God-given message with truth and power, and make it speak to the minds of modern men. What is needed is a much closer linkage of evangelism with theology, and a recognition of the interplay of divine with human factors in both spheres.

The bedrock of Christian faith is that God was in Jesus Christ, speaking to men and acting for men with revealing light and saving power. The Christian gospel, whether as revelation or redemption, comes to us from God by his will and purpose, and is not merely of our own devising. Moral endeavors in response to the gospel, like theologies which attempt to clarify and systematize its truth, are man-made structures; the gospel is from beyond ourselves. Yet in laying hold of it, both for the renewal of life and the apprehension of truth, human co-operation is necessary. God neither saves nor informs us passively. He gives new life and imparts some measure of his truth to our minds only when we are open to receive it and willing to pay the cost of clear thinking and devoted living.

Furthermore, God imparts his truth and power, not in the abstract, but always within a concrete human situation. What he has given us in Christ is a timeless gospel, but it always comes to us in time and must be transmitted in time, within the conditions of a particular age and social climate. This makes it imperative to see as clearly as possible our human opportunities and human predicament, and try to discern what God is saying to us in the midst of it. Tentatively as far as our own human wisdom is concerned—but confident in the assurance that in Christ, God has spoken and is speaking to our age—we must try to discover, to understand, and to proclaim the gospel.

We shall therefore attempt now to broaden the scope of our inquiry in two directions. We shall first ask what are the deepest desires of the modern man—of persons in the churches, on their margins, and outside of all religious bodies. In short, what are the elemental promptings of the human spirit as they appear within the conditions of our time in the Western world? We shall then in a quick survey attempt to consider some of the things which the churches have to say to the modern mind from the eternal truths of the Christian faith.

What are the deepest desires of the modern man? Amid confusion and chaos in the outward scene, disharmony among the nations, high prices and high wages and high taxes, uncertainty as to the political or economic future, what would modern man like most to have?

He would of course like to see peace and prosperity upon earth. But there are other things he thinks more about. He wants to possess, to enjoy, to be admired and looked up to. In this he is like all his ancestors, though there are now many more things to possess and more apparent sources of enjoyment. He wants to have and to enjoy what he wants to without restriction from the government or any other quarter. He does not want to be tied down by too little money, or too long hours of work, or too constricting traditions. He wants a family, for considerations in which biological impulse, desire for companionship, and genuine love play a mixed role; and he wants his family to have what they need for their comfort and social standing. He wants a decent job that will give him an assured income. Within the intersecting circles of the job, the family, and personal desires, the modern individual's world is focused.

In short, modern man wants to be his own master. But the way is not easy going. Attainable as are some of these desires, the network is so complex that he finds them frequently in conflict. He cannot get ahead in business and do all the other things he wants to; he cannot always please his family and please himself. He tries to "have his cake and eat it," but it does not work. Some of his desires are opposed by moral considerations which, though he tries not to be bound by old-fashioned scruples, he can neither obey nor silence. Many of his wishes as soon as they are fulfilled turn to emptiness or evoke a more intense longing for something else.

As a result frustration has become not only a familiar term but a familiar experience in our time. Frustration is not new to human nature; but as life becomes more complex and the means of satisfying material desires more numerous and alluring, frustration at failure to find the deeper satisfactions increases proportionately.

When modern man tries to have his own way and finds that the world does not respond readily to his wishes, he pities himself, gets nervous, and looks for a way of escape. The particular route that is followed depends much on temperament and the social situation. Among the commonest routes are alcohol, sexual variety, speeding on the highways, exciting sports or movies or radio or wood pulp, harder work with less time to think, the physician, the psychiatrist, some cult or other.

What the modern man is looking for, though he often fails to realize it, is dependable sources of inner satisfaction. It is these which the Christian religion has given to men for nineteen centuries and can give to men today.

What can the Christian religion contribute to our baffled world? The answer is found in the last verse of the thirteenth chapter of I Corinthians, "So faith, hope, love abide, these three; but the greatest of these is love.

Overshadowing and permeating every desire mentioned above is the desire for *security*. Modern man wants to be secure from annihilation by atomic bombs and economic loss. He wants security and prestige for his family. He lauds the goals of freedom from fear and want in the world scene, though he is less willing to pay the price of their achievement. But beneath all other longings for security is his desire to be free from fear and inferiority and conflict within, to find meaning in life and a power to live by, to find a home for his soul. In short he wants a *faith* that will see him through.

Modern man in the midst of much that is shaky and uncertain wants *confidence* in something. He does not have much confidence in the United Nations, in the politicians who run the government, or even in military force, though he does not see what else to depend on if things get worse. He would like to trust the scientists to create a brave new world; but though he trusts them more than others, he is not sure they are equal to it. He may or may not have confidence in his personal family ties, but the termination of one marriage in every four by divorce does not strengthen his assurance. He would like to project his life into the future through his children, but he does not know whether they will be left alive a generation hence. He desperately needs *hope* but finds little of which to be hopeful.

Modern man wants *fellowship.* In spite of some satisfactions within the family and the circle of his friends he is on the whole a lonely creature. Technology and the accompanying competitive struggle make for much togetherness but little understanding or sharing of life. Overcrowding and the unremitting pressures of space and time increase the degree to which one is jostled, body and soul, but decrease the opportunity of unhurried and fruitful communion with other souls. The family is a scene of tension perhaps more often than of fellowship. Relatively few people, whether children or adults, feel themselves to be deeply loved or fully understood. It is apparent that modern man for his soul's survival needs not only faith and hope but *love*.

The Christian religion has the answer to this predicament. "So faith, hope, love abide, these three; but the greatest of these is love."

In what, then, can the Christian have faith? For what can he hope? How can he love and be loved?

Our first answer must be *faith in the living God* in whom, and in whom alone, is man's true security. But what may a Christian believe about God?

It is the Christian faith that God is the creator and ruler of the universe, a righteous and loving Father who demands goodness in his children, a saving God who in mercy forgives the penitent sinner and gives him a new start in life. God is both within and beyond the currents of history and human destiny; and while his will may be thwarted, he cannot finally be defeated. His will, discoverable in Jesus Christ, is for peace, righteousness, reconciliation, and "the abundant life" among men.

Each of these concepts has profound bearing upon the plight of modern man, and more clearly grasped and appropriated could remake our world.

To say that God is the creator and ruler of the universe is to exalt him above the world and its manifold claims. It is to regard not mechanical force but spiritual personality as the ultimate in existence, and to put physical things in their rightful place as servant, not master, of the spirit. Science, whether descriptive science or applied science, can live in harmony with religious faith if the discovery of natural law is the charting of God's ways of working and if technology means the production of goods for the enlargement of men's capacities as God's servants. Once more an ancient word becomes relevant, "Thou shalt have no other gods before me."

To say that God is a righteous and loving Father who demands goodness in his children is to affirm the existence of a moral order in the universe, the operation of which, though less precise, is as certain as any physical law. The world is so made that men cannot sin with impunity, as the events of recent years have clearly shown. This is true whether the sin is the selfishness and self-righteousness of the individual human spirit or the collective sin of global destruction. But God is not judge only; he is Father. This means that all men are meant by God to be brothers; and because we *are* brothers, we ought to treat one another as such. Before this conviction, if taken seriously, no race prejudice, no economic strife, no national arrogance could stand.

To say that God gives saving help to the shattered, the empty, the vacillating, the sinful life is to say that what has happened to many millions of individuals in Christian history can happen to any individual today. This "good news" of the Christian gospel is that if one is willing to pay the price of obedience and moral surrender, God can take any life and make it over. To find such saving help is to find a new center for the soul, new direction, new power, new joy. It is what our baffled, frustrated modern man with his welter of conflicting desires needs most.

To say that the eternal God is the Lord of history also is to say that "in his will is our peace." There is no guarantee that man may not destroy himself in total war. Yet of two things the Christian can be confident: that the way of brotherhood and mutual understanding is God's way, which if followed leads to justice, security, and peace; and that if man does end his collective life upon earth, God will still reign in his eternal Kingdom. This assurance affords no naïve optimism, but in it the Christian can labor, and pray, and wait in hope.

Faith in the living God of Christian faith provides a ground of security, of confidence, of fellowship with the Most High. But how may the Christian know that this faith is not simply "a lurking luminosity, a cosy thought"? The answer is in *what we see of God in Jesus Christ,* and in the grounds of *hope* he sets before us.

Among the various and sometimes conflicting doctrines which the churches have held regarding Christ, two stand out as central. These are that he is the revealer of God and the redeemer of men.

In the self-giving, impartial love of Jesus, in his compassion, understanding, eagerness to heal the bodies and souls of men, in deeds of love during his ministry and the supreme sacrifice of the Cross, we see what God is and what he is always doing for men. Though the details of Christian living are not neatly charted for us in the Sermon on the Mount or elsewhere, we are left in no doubt as to the type of character and action which God as seen in Jesus requires of us. Complex as life is, to evade Christian decision on the basis of inadequate direction from Jesus is to evade moral responsibility on other grounds. In his teaching and example of unbroken fellowship with God, of love and service to men, of humility and sincerity, of forgiveness toward even his most malicious enemies, of sensitive understanding of the spoken or unspoken needs of the humblest of persons whose lives touched his, we see the kind of living to which we are called. This is something very different from the selfish, callously indifferent, thing-centered desire for personal enjoyment which so widely pervades modern life.

But to know through Jesus what God requires of us is not to do it! Awareness of this fact is important, but it need not foredoom us to despair. For at the heart of Christian faith is the gospel of divine grace, and the conviction that in Jesus Christ is not the *pattern* only, but the *power* for man's salvation. In him God has acted, not to make us sinless, but to lift the burden of our sin and give us victory. Not only through the ministry of his words and works, but through his death in apparent defeat and the triumph of his resurrection to be with us always as a Living Presence, God has acted for our healing. It is an ever-repeated miracle that to those who commit their lives to Christ in loyalty and faith God gives forgiveness of sin and deliverance from frustration and fear. What man must do is to open the channels of the soul through repentance and humble submission to God. What God does is to make life over until one becomes a new creature in Christ Jesus, victorious and strong. The kind of living that eventuates is described by Paul, "The fruit of the Spirit is love, joy, peace, patience, kindness, goodness, faithfulness, gentleness, self-control; against such there is no law."

The new life in Christ is not without its continuing costs. It must be nourished in prayer. It calls for more kindness, sympathy, and sharing—in short, more love—within the family, in business, toward other races, toward our enemies, among the world's suffering multitudes. This is not easy. But who would not gladly exchange the kind of society we have for such a fellowship?

This brings us to the third great need of modern man—the need for *love* to prevail, and strife and enmity to be done away with. Human nature being what it is, is there any prospect that this may come to pass? What is the Christian view of *man?*

The Christian judgment regarding man's nature is twofold, and both aspects need continually to be kept in mind. The first and last word, ranging in the Bible from the majestic symbolism of the Genesis story of creation to other great imagery in the book of Revelation, is that man is a spiritual creature, made in the divine likeness, the child of God and intended by God for eternity. Yet on almost every page of the Bible is the record of human sin and rebellion, and the need of divine forgiveness and saving help because man is not good enough or wise enough or strong enough to save himself.

What is written in the Bible is written everywhere in human experience. There are marks of the divine image in the kindness, generosity, self-forgetfulness, and high devotion of which even common men are capable. Yet men can be indescribably brutal, vindictive, arrogant, and hard. War brings out both sets of qualities. But the best of men in the best times are sinners, desiring at some points to have their own way and exalt themselves above God and their fellow men. There is no one who, if he is honest with himself, does not need to say, "God, be merciful to me a sinner."

The Christian conception of man as a child of God, as was intimated earlier, has profound social significance. The basic ground of democracy is this belief in the innate worth and dignity of every human creature, regardless of race, color, nation, economic status, language, creed, culture, or any other man-made line of cleavage. This is the chief meeting point of the Church with men of good will outside its ranks.

General recognition of this essential equality of men is the only hope for a just and peaceful world. From the Christian perspective the way out of our present social confusion lies neither in relying on military force nor sacrificing principle for appeasement, neither in fighting a "cold war" nor in yielding to totalitarian autocracy. It lies rather in respecting the men of all nations and peoples as sons of God and, as sons of God and forgiven sinners ourselves, trying humbly and without malice to do the works of healing, relief, and reconciliation which are the will of God.

Yet in this needful emphasis on the dignity of man—and of all men—the Christian conception of man as sinner ought never to be forgotten. To do so is to blind ourselves to our own evil and impotence. Any form of theology or of preaching which moves lightly over the stark fact of sin is foredoomed by its shallow optimism to the failure which awaits too great lightheartedness in a tragic world. God has given man dominion "over the fish of the sea, and over the fowl of the air, and over every living thing that moveth upon the earth"—and we may add, over steam, electricity, ether waves, the stratosphere, plutonium, uranium, and every invisible physical power. But God has not given man dominion over his own soul, to save himself by his own goodness or wisdom from either inner dissolution or outward destruction. God alone in divine love empowers man to confront his world, and God in Christ points the way.

This in brief is the gospel of faith and hope and love, mediated to man from God through Jesus Christ, which the churches hold in their keeping. It is this gospel which the churches must offer to the people if they are to justify their existence and fulfill their divine mission. Amid much bad news this "good news" is what the world needs above all else. With it modern man can live and face the future with security, confidence, fellowship with God and man. Without it the outlook for faith or hope or love, whether in the individual soul or the social scene, is nebulous and dark.

CHAPTER III

The Gospel in the Churches

UP TO THIS POINT we have used the terms "Church" and "the churches" almost interchangeably, assuming that the Church is the corporate name for the churches. It now becomes necessary to draw sharper distinctions. Our inquiry in this chapter will aim to make some assessment of three dominant types of American church life in terms of their success in inculcating personal religion and communicating the gospel for the upbuilding of vital Christian experience. The types we shall examine are the Roman Catholic, the fundamentalist Protestant, and the liberal Protestant.[1]

Since a discussion of this sort so easily runs into generalities, some definitions are required at the start. Indeed, even with the definitions generalizations will be inevitable, for there is no precise measuring rod for Christian experience, and in the nature of the case no statistics are procurable.

As we shall use the term, "personal Christian living"

[1] The Eastern Orthodox type, though an important part of ecumenical Christianity, is numerically so much in the minority in the United States that it is not included in this discussion.

is marked by a conscious reference of the life of the individual to God, both for divine support and in a sincere desire to discover and do the will of God as revealed in Christ. The term "Christian," which we use so glibly, is not easy to define. It cannot be equated with church membership, or with adherence to conventional moral demands, or with a flash-in-the-pan conversion experience if the life of the individual is not made better by it. Perhaps the simplest and most inclusive definition is that a Christian is a person who sincerely tries to be a follower of Jesus.

This is not to say that anyone completely succeeds in the attempt to be a follower of Jesus. "The sin which doth so easily beset us" stands ever in the way, even for the best; and it is a common fact that the best Christians are apt to be more conscious of their sins than those who are lukewarm. Yet to be a Christian, if the experience is real, makes a difference. The life of the Christian is distinguished by an inner peace, joy, serenity, sense of direction, and triumph over adversity that transforms the individual's personality. If this inward experience is deep and genuine, his life is marked outwardly by an unselfish concern for others and desire to help them in any way that is possible, by courage in making hard moral decisions, by an integrity which goes much deeper than conventional honesty in the eyes of the law. It is impossible to draw up a list of character traits and say that all those possessing them are Christians while all others are not. Life comes too mixed for that. Yet as one thinks of persons he knows to be unmistakably Christian, a certain pattern and quality of life are distinguishable, more readily discerned by acquaintance than defined in words, which give meaning and content to the term "personal Christian living."

A preliminary word is also in order as to the three main types of American Christianity we propose to look at. That one treads on dangerous ground here is evident, for tensions are acute and misunderstandings are easy. Let it be said at the start, therefore, that I have no desire to stigmatize or laud any type, but only to give as fair an appraisal as possible with the hope of seeing what can be learned from types other than our own.

The Roman Catholic type requires no definition. By the fundamentalist Protestant type we mean those churches which hold to the verbal inspiration and hence the literal inerrancy of the Bible, and which defend as of vital importance certain creedal dogmas, notably the virgin birth, the blood atonement, the physical resurrection of Christ, and his visible second coming. By liberal Protestantism we mean those churches which stress the historical approach to the Bible and hence its spiritual rather than literal inspiration, and find the source of Christian authority not in any creedal statement but in God's total and progressive revelation of himself in nature, history, human experience, and supremely in Jesus Christ. The Roman Catholic and the fundamentalist Protestant positions, though with obvious differences, meet in holding to an authoritarian and traditionalist point of view as over against the liberal emphasis on free inquiry. These types of Protestantism cut across not only denominations but local congregations, for not infrequently the laity are prevailingly fundamentalist while the minister is liberal. There are many churches and some individuals that cannot easily be classified. Yet there are recognizable prevailing trends, and with due allowance for overlapping at the edges certain observations may be made.

There is both truth and falsehood in the assertion frequently made, that if one wants to find virility and power in Christianity today, he has to go to the Roman Catholic or to the fundamentalist Protestant churches to find it. That there is enough truth in it to give sober concern to others is attested by the almost universal witness of the chaplains during the war. Both the Catholics and the members of fundamentalist groups seemed to take their religion more seriously than the rank and file of service men brought up in liberal Protestant homes and churches. Not only did they attend chapel more faithfully, but they seemed to have more to rely on in time of crisis. And they knew far more definitely what they believed, the religious illiteracy of men from the major Protestant churches being one of the most conspicuous and startling discoveries of the war experience. To move to a different sphere of witness, I can testify from nearly twenty years of college teaching that the students likely to resist the inroads of secularism, and to maintain a warm interest in religion when the pull of the college community is in another direction, are most often those from Catholic and conservative Protestant homes. Those in the latter group not infrequently break with their parents' theology to move to a more liberal outlook, but it is significant that they have something to move *from.*

A more telling form of witness lies in the realm of intangibles. Among the professing Christians we know, who is able best to take calamity without being floored by it and, whatever happens, go forward with faith that all is safe in the hands of God? Who finds from his religion greater staying power in the face of what he recognizes as moral temptation? Who takes his religion seriously enough to attend church when it is highly inconvenient? Who puts himself out most to see that his children receive religious instruction? There is no possibility of flat generalizations here, for some persons in each type rank high and others low. Nevertheless, it is my conviction that in most of these questions the scales are tipped on the side of the authoritarian types of Christianity.

In any case there is no clear evidence that liberal Christianity is superior in its personal fruits, and there are some indices to the contrary. This does *not* mean, as some might superficially conclude, that the liberal approach is thus proved false, and that the ground it has gained during the past century in the quest for a freer source of authority in Christian truth ought to be surrendered. It means only that if the Roman Catholics or the fundamentalist Protestants have any real achievements which liberal Protestantism lacks, we had better find out what they are, and why, and what is to be done about it.

If the conservative churches are producing more personal religious vitality than the others, the explanation is not likely to be found in one quarter only. The primary factors which bear on the question seem to me to be five: (1) the churchgoing habit in these churches is earlier and more persistently associated with religion; (2) the emotional accompaniments of worship are more vivid and dramatic; (3) greater demands—or at least, greater consciously recognized demands—are made on church members; (4) more concrete instruction is given in Christian doctrine; and (5) in spite of some false notes, other notes are struck which in certain great essentials lie closer to the heart of the Christian gospel than the usual liberal emphasis. Each of these matters requires further examination.

In the first place, for the development of personal religious living and the inculcation of loyalty both to Christ and his church, when ought children to begin going to church? I do not mean going to the church school, or the boys' or girls' club which meets at the church, or to the daily vacation Bible school in the summer vacation. All of these if properly conducted have a highly useful function. But I am asking a more radical question. When ought a child to begin attending the Sunday morning service of worship? In general the Roman Catholic and many of the more conservative Protestants begin taking their children to church as soon as they are able to sit through a service without making a public disturbance. In the Catholic fold a child by the age of seven has usually made his first communion, and the obligations of regular attendance at mass are as binding on him as on his elders. Protestants vary widely, but the more sophisticated the church the more likely the assumption that the church service is for adults only, and the children either do not go to church at all or leave before the sermon.

This latter practice we have adopted from a prevalent psychological assumption, namely, that a child will be so bored by the church service that he will be injured in his psyche and perhaps alienated from religion by being forced to submit to it. This assumption I regard as false and disastrous to both the child and the Church. A truer psychology affirms that what is put into the first of life is put into the whole of life, and that very little *does* get into the whole of life which does not have its roots in the early years. Probably most of you who read these pages, like me, began going to church longer ago than you can remember. I doubt that it ever hurt us; and if we had not begun young, we probably should not now be caring much either about the Church or about reading books on the Christian religion.

Second, what ought the service of worship to do for the worshiper? It ought clearly to lift him into the presence of God, make him feel the sustaining power of God, stir him to self-examination of his own moral life, send him out with a sense of joy and peace to better living. The two prevailing types of cultus in Christian churches are liturgical and sermon-centered, corresponding roughly to the Catholic and Protestant traditions though with no clear demarcation between them. The liturgical type centers in the "objective" worship of God, with the primary focus on what God has done for men in the sending of his son Jesus Christ for our redemption and the continued mediation of divine grace through the Church. The architecture of the church is designed to accent this note, with the altar in the center and much use of the church's historic symbols. Whether or not a mass is celebrated, what is done in such a service is usually done with beauty, dignity, and reverence. The sensuous imagery of vestments, candles, bells, and other physical media of worship, the solemn hush of the assembly as the prayers of the ages are said, the bowed head, the bended knee, the music which is never frolicsome but searching in its simple cadences—all this tends to produce an impression of worship which even without much ideological content is deep and compelling. Protestants often assume that Catholics go to church only because of fear and ecclesiastical compulsion. Rather it needs to be asked whether it is not the combination of a deep-seated churchgoing habit with such use of drama appealing to the imagination which keeps so many Roman Catholics faithfully attending church while their Protestant friends stay at home for a long Sunday morning snooze.

But what of Protestant worship? It of course takes many forms too numerous to describe.[2] What is most noteworthy from the standpoint of our present concern is that fundamentalist Protestant worship, though at opposite poles from the type just mentioned, has great similarities in its basic appeals. If one goes to a tabernacle or tent meeting, he hears jingly "gospel" songs, animated tones, shouts from the preacher, and frequent "Amens" or other more pointed ejaculations from the pews. There is much personal testimony, and the success of the meeting is judged mainly by the number of conversions it brings about. This intensely personal, apparently spontaneous action under the power of the Holy Spirit seems far removed from the sober dignity of a liturgical service. Yet in both there are strong sensuous appeals, expression of the religious life through

[2] An important type is the silent worship of the Friends' Meeting, in which there are often both a high expectancy and discovery of the Divine Presence. It is omitted here because the chapter attempts to discuss only the three most prevalent types of churches.

dramatic familiar forms, group reinforcement of a dominant idea, and something for the congregation themselves to do. Compare either type with the dignified but largely colorless conventional Protestant service in which the would-be worshipers sing perfunctorily, sit woolgathering through the prayer, and listen passively while the preacher discourses moral platitudes which most of them have heard all their lives—and it is not surprising that Rome and the sects seem to be winning out.

But, in the third place, what do the churches ask their people to do? This question may be asked in several senses—either about what is required to be done in the church service, or in the service of the Church, or in the service of God and one's neighbor under the impulsion of the Church. It requires, therefore, several different answers.

Within the service of worship itself much is required of the worshiper in the Catholic service by way of kneeling, standing, saying responses, genuflection, and making the sign of the cross. There is no opportunity, however much one may desire to, to go to sleep; and while there is no sure preventive to mind-wandering, the service through centuries of tradition has been so formulated as to require a considerable degree of attention. In the more emotional types of Protestant service both the external stimuli and the inner warmth which the worshiper expects—and goes to church to secure—are conducive to attention. Indeed, so captivated is his attention that he may find himself shouting and leaping for joy without realizing he is doing so. In our more formal sermon-centered services little is required of the worshiper except to sit decorously, stand, and bow his head at appropriate intervals, and rare indeed is the minister who can capture his roving thoughts all the time from eleven o'clock until twelve-fifteen.

From the standpoint of duties owed to the Church, the Roman Catholic churchman again is in a favored position in that he knows definitely what is expected of him. He must attend mass once every Sunday and on specified holy days; he must eat no meat on Friday; he must confess his sins at intervals; he must see that the children are baptized, instructed, and confirmed in the Catholic faith; he must perform his Easter duties; he must give generously to the church, the amount or the proportion of his income being perhaps specified by the priest. There is no guesswork as to what is required; and if he is a "good Catholic," he does all of these things without a great deal of rebellion. Protestants may scoff at the artificiality of it, but there is a form of moral discipline here which ought not to be surrendered without more vital substitutes.

Protestantism, whether conservative or liberal, has far less explicit religious duties; but in what is required in money-giving, money-raising by church activities, and the carrying on of the church's voluntary organizations there is a source not only of power for the church but of growth for the church member. It is a great disadvantage for any church to be heavily endowed, and virile Christianity is seldom found therein. This is no small part of the reason why the American churches, with all their weakness, are in general in a healthier condition than the state-supported churches of Europe. Laywomen are generally closer to the life of the church than are the laymen, not because they are essentially better Christians, but because they find more to do in the church's voluntary organizations. Young people not put to work are often lost to the Church, and this is one main reason for the heavy leakage in the college and immediately postcollege years. "Spectatoritis" in any church is a dangerous malady, which has been greatly intensified of late years by the prevailing practice of securing a speaker for every occasion instead of using local effort and initiative in preparing a program.

It is at the point of what the Church requires of—or at least enjoins upon—its members in the total social situation that the liberal churches compare most favorably with the other two. This is our hope; is it fulfilled? Theological conservatism often, though not always, goes hand in hand with social conservatism. Ministers trained in liberal seminaries usually have a more informed and sensitive conscience about the bearing of Christianity on major social problems. Some of them preach in these terms with great prophetic passion and power. Yet the troublesome fact that confronts us is that so many seem mainly to preach inoffensive moral injunctions, and apparently pride themselves on keeping their congregations from discovering that in the seminary they acquired any new ideas! One listens to such a sermon and goes away feeling, "That is true, but what of it?" The reasons are doubtless many, and they center in human nature rather than in liberal theology. Conservatism gives tough resistance; the effort follows an uphill road; the minister has the duty to be tactful as well as courageous—and before long he is saying things so flattened out as to offend nobody. The Mr. Browns and Mr. Smiths listen politely, and go home to keep up with the Joneses.

Whether the laity in prevailingly liberal churches can be shown to have more sensitive consciences than others and a greater sense of compulsion in serving their fellow men, I do not know. The cultural level is generally higher, but culture is not Christianity. The much-publicized poll reported in the November, 1948, issue of the *Ladies' Home Journal* [3] could have thrown light on this question if closer correlations had been drawn between the replies to theological and ethical questions; but as the report stands, a very general state of complacency and self-satisfaction is indicated regardless of religious background. The most that can be said with certainty is that while liberal preaching specializes on

[3] "God and the American People" by Lincoln Barnett.

the moral aspects of Christianity, there is no clear indication that higher moral fruits are obtained.

Whether or not there is actually a connection between theology and morals, there ought to be; and if we were giving the right teaching in both fields, there would be. What then, in the fourth place, can be said comparatively regarding instruction in the truths of the Christian faith?

It must be said frankly that no one of the types of churches we are considering is doing a highly commendable job at this point. Roman Catholic children have to learn their catechisms before they are confirmed, and those who attend parochial schools receive more instruction in doctrine, as well as in the practices of their church, than Protestant children generally get. But this is not to say that they understand what it means. In fact they are commonly encouraged not to try to understand the mysteries of the faith. Conservative Protestants believe strongly in a limited circle of ideas and know how to quote texts freely in support of them, but again this is not to say that there is any comprehensive grasp of the issues involved.

Both of these authoritarian groups are ahead of the liberals in the concreteness of their religious instruction, as well as probably in its amount. Despite the great emphasis on religious education in the liberal churches during the past fifty years, the religious illiteracy of the general public has increased rather than diminished

that doesn't interfere with his friendship with Joe Doakes, who is an equally staunch Democrat. He was as startled as anybody else at the way the election went, and it looks to him as if we are in for a lot more government spending and waste of the taxpayer's good money. But what he cannot understand is why anybody should be enough of a crackpot to vote for Norman Thomas, or why any real American should be in love with the Russians enough to vote for Henry Wallace. Capitalism has its flaws, of course, but preachers had better keep their hands off what they do not know much about.

Mr. Brown believes in racial equality. He always has. The minister preached a fine sermon not long ago on the brotherhood of man, and he agreed with every word of it. It is terrible how the Nazis treated the Jews. The British had no business to stay in India as long as they did. The people of every country ought to be free. The Negroes here are all right as long as they keep their place. But the way both they and the Jews are trying to push themselves in and get jobs and buy property is a caution! You have to keep your eyes open, or they will work their way in and run you out.

Mr. Brown contributes generously, both to the church budget and to other good causes like the Red Cross and the Community Chest. In the latter he is particularly glad to contribute to a Community Club for Negro boys and girls. He does not want them at the "Y" swimming pool with his children; and besides, the missus may be right in what she says about the danger of intermarriage.

He is glad to give something, too, to help the starving in war-devastated lands. He is essentially a kind man and does not like to think of anybody's having to go hungry. However, he thinks the minister has rather overdone his appeals to send food to the Germans. After all, they started it, and it will not hurt them to have a little dose of their own medicine.

We can give only a passing look at certain other of Mr. Brown's interests. There is his lodge, which he is sure has as much religion in it as the churches, and if one lived up to it he would not need the church. When the meeting of the official board of the church was accidentally placed on the same night as the Masons', he was in a tight spot but decided the lodge needed him more because the minister was paid to run the church. There is also his service club, at which he never misses a Wednesday luncheon. His club does a lot of good by contributing to a hospital for crippled children, and anyway there is one place where you can get away from the women and be a man!

Other forms of recreation less void of female influence are the dinners and evenings of bridge to which his wife escorts him. He does not really care much about them—is too tired after the day's work—but if you are a family man there are some things you have to put up with. If and when cocktails are served, he has to drink a little, not because he likes it but because nobody wants to be a wet blanket. On other occasions when he is among church people who do not drink, the conversation readily turns upon the badness of those who do. Mr. Brown adapts himself as best he can to either situation.

We must now leave Mr. Brown with his private moral and social dilemmas. Several observations are in order.

A first observation may be needed to counteract any impression that the foregoing description of Mr. Brown is an attempt to decry or ridicule the layman's situation. If he fails to let his economic or political life be guided primarily by the Christian gospel, it is not because he is bad, unintelligent, or essentially weak. He merits sympathy rather than blame; and if he keeps his connection with the church enough to support it by his attendance and contributions, in spite of what must seem to him the irrelevance of many of its activities, he deserves much credit. Viewing himself, he ought to realize that he could be and ought to be a better Christian in his business and civic life than he is. Viewed by his minister, he ought to be seen for what he is—a man caught in a situation so different from the minister's that only by the most unusual discernment can he possibly look at the social scene from the minister's point of view.

A second observation is the main theme of this book

—that if the layman's life is to be radically affected by the Christian gospel, the Christian faith must be communicated to him in language that he can understand. He hears in church a great many platitudes and familiar moral exhortations which do not move him much, with now and then a sermon which gives great comfort and support to the inner life. He hears, at least in some churches, words about sin, repentance, forgiveness, atonement, incarnation, redemption, the kingdom of heaven, eternal life, the grace of God and the saving power of the living Christ. What this has to do with him, or with the world of sharp competition and rising prices, he has only the vaguest notion. The minister might as well be talking Greek or Hebrew. That such terms stand for ideas which have any bearing on the world in which he moves six days of the week and most of the seventh would be a startling discovery. It is a discovery he is not likely to make unless theologians and ministers do a much better job than we have thus far in stating the eternal truths of the Christian faith in language both simple and relevant to the layman's world.

A primary principle of educational psychology is the law of apperception; nothing has meaning until it is apperceived in terms of what has already been experienced and known. This law we violate continually in our preaching. There is no more pertinent verse in the Bible than that which says, "And I sat where he sat."

We cannot expect the layman to see the gospel from the minister's point of view until the minister sees the world through the layman's eyes.

But in the third place, the layman himself must do something about the situation. It is not all his fault, but neither is he the helpless victim of circumstances. We can do no more here than to suggest the direction that needs to be taken. The way out lies along the channels of fellowship, study, action, prayer, and personal witness.

Most learning is done in a social situation, where those of kindred interests unite to learn from a common source or—often more effectively—from one another in a pooling of insights and experience. This is as true of adult learning and of Christian learning as any other, but it is a principle we have hardly begun to apply to the problem now under consideration. Only as laymen decide they care enough about the applications of the Christian faith to unite in study under leadership, or to unite in discussion to learn from one another in a fellowship, are we apt to get far toward bridging the gap between the Church and the world.

Sermons and ministerially-led discussion groups are not useless. But they are likely to be far less useful than serious study initiated and carried through by laymen themselves. This is for two reasons: first, the minister by the detachment of his vocation knows less about the layman's problems than laymen do; and second, such groups too easily run into one more discourse to which by long conditioning it is customary to listen passively without being very much stirred to action.

But can laymen be aroused to initiate or participate in studies of the relation of the gospel to their jobs? In Europe it has been done far more extensively than here. The Ecumenical Institute of the World Council of Churches at the Chateau de Bossey near Geneva has as one of its major functions the bringing together of groups of people of a common profession—Christian doctors, lawyers, educators, industrialists, political leaders—for a week or ten days of mutual probing of the applications of Christian faith to their vocations. A similar enterprise at the Evangelical Academy at Bad Boll, near Stuttgart, Germany, has made a significant start toward bridging the gap between the Church and the industrial worker by inviting representatives of the Trade Unions and Workers' Councils, including sometimes communists, to discuss the implications of Christianity, while on other occasions employers and Workers' Council leaders have met together for mutual discussion of the applications of the gospel to industry. Perhaps better known is the Iona Community, where on an island off the coast of Scotland a group consisting half of theological students or young ministers and half of artisans live and work together during the summer months, leading a life of discipline and prayer as they jointly rebuild the ruined medieval abbey. Other such projects are the Sigtuna Institute in Sweden, the Kerk en Wereld center near Utrecht in Holland, Cluny in France, the Zoë movement in Greece, and numerous other less permanent arrangements by which Christian laymen meet occasionally for a week end of conference on matters of mutual Christian concern.[1] Though our distances are greater in America, so are our financial resources; and there is no reason why similar projects should not be developed here if laymen saw the need and value of a shared inquiry as to what Christianity actually means in the daily job.

But obviously such conferences, though they can be enormously stimulating and eye-opening, are not enough. What can be done in the local church?

The fellowship principle can be joined with study, action, and prayer in the small, informal, self-conducted group which for lack of a better name is usually called a cell group. Elton Trueblood in *Alternative to Futility* calls it "the fellowship of the concerned." Its main idea is a co-operative inquiry and sharing of experience along

[1] For a fuller account of these projects see *Centers of New Life in European Christendom* by Walter M. Horton, which may be secured from the American Office of the World Council of Churches, 297 Fourth Ave., New York. Descriptions of several of them are to be found in issues of the *Christian Century* for Sept. 11, 1946, Jan. 22, 1947, August 18, 1948, and Sept. 1, 1948. See also *We Shall Re-build* by George MacLeod (American edition published by Kirkridge, 808 Witherspoon Building, Philadelphia, Pa.) for a description of the philosophy and work of the Iona Community.

some line of mutual concern, with meetings at regular intervals and often with self-imposed disciplines. The cell idea is not to be recommended unreservedly, for it has in it dangers as well as values. Cell groups can be harmful when they withdraw from the main stream of the Church, become ingrowing, adopt a "holier than thou" attitude. Nevertheless, they can be vitally helpful when they are an integral part of church life and their members are humble, seeking, vitally concerned Christians. In the sharing of Christian experience and mutual reinforcement in the faith the idea has affinities with the Methodist class meetings of an earlier day; and when the cell principle is integrated sufficiently with the rest of life, it reminds one of those early Christian groups who "day by day, attending the temple together and breaking bread in their homes, . . . partook of food with glad and generous hearts, praising God and having favor with all the people." [2] Vital interest in a cell group can never be superimposed; but if a co-operative search for the bearing of the gospel on daily life seems a matter of great importance, a place may well be found for it even if it means the elimination of something else from crowded schedules.

Reference has been made to the need not only of fellowship and study but of prayer and action. These are too large themes for detailed discussion at this point.

[2] Acts 2:46-47 (R.S.V.).

Yet clearly both are of such paramount importance that we shall not make much headway without them. It needs to be stressed that neither prayer nor action can be very effective unless each is reinforced by the other. Though there ought to be no oversimplification of either the Christian ethic or the devotional life, a good share of our perplexities in both fields would disappear with a more active conjunction of the two. If we do not "pray without ceasing" for a better society and seize every opportunity however slight to act on the side of the ends we pray for, the power of God is apt to sound like melodious words and the resources of men seem wholly inadequate to cope with the difficulties. This is another way of saying that we must try to find the gospel in its fullness if it is to be very effective anywhere.

Laymen need not be daunted in this undertaking. Even in the absence of organized effort by church leaders there are enormously important things which any layman can do to discover, to act upon, and to communicate the gospel.

We have said repeatedly that the Christian faith is both something to be believed and something to be lived; it is both truth and power. For the gospel as a body of belief there are books available; and while few can take a full course in theology, anyone who can read the English language can find out, if he cares to, what the basic tenets of the Christian faith are.[3] The discovery costs something, but it is a cost which any person can meet by earnest inquiry.

The faith to be lived is far more costly. It is at this point above all others that he who would have it must give it. We have scarcely touched the possibilities of lay witness to the gospel within the conditions of the common life, and we are not likely to have any far-reaching, deep-going evangelism until laymen realize that it is their responsibility, and not the minister's only, to present the living realities of the gospel to their fellows and win them to Christ. One of the most trenchant statements in the Amsterdam Report is that which says, "The Church must find its way to the places where men really live. It must penetrate the alienated world from within, and make the minds of men familiar with the elementary realities of God, of sin, and of purpose in life." This the Church is not very likely to do unless laymen give their witness in the midst of their daily tasks.

Such witness takes many forms.[4] There is no "rule

[3] For a bibliography of relatively simple books on basic Christian beliefs consult the appendix of my *Understanding the Christian Faith*. To the list there given should be added three excellent books that have appeared since it was published, H. F. Rall's *The Christian Faith and Way* (Abingdon-Cokesbury, 1947), James H. Nichols' *Primer for Protestants* (Association Press, 1947), and Nels Ferré's *Pillars of Faith* (Harper, 1948).

[4] For a description of many forms of witness by both clergy and laity see the chapter entitled "The Gospel at Work in the World" in Volume II of the Amsterdam Series, *The Church's Witness to God's Design*.

of thumb" for doing it. Unctuous piety must be avoided. Often the most effective witness is that which emerges naturally in the human situation when issues arise and decisions must be made in which one can either drift with the tide or take a forthright Christian stand. When a person is unmistakably Christian, his neighbors and associates will find it out, and there is a sense in which it is true that what one does speaks louder than what he says. But such unconscious, unspoken witness ought never to be an alibi or substitute for the spoken word on occasions when speech is appropriate. Witness we must, by word and deed, if the gospel is to mean anything more to the world around us than an inherited body of moral platitudes, eminently respectable but of doubtful practicality.

Will such witness be heard and heeded in our time? The obstacles are great, but there is no need to despair. The Christian gospel, both as truth and power, is intended for all men. There is nothing esoteric about it, and it is the testimony of the ages that "whosoever will may come." There is no race or nation, no economic, cultural, or social stratum where the doors are impenetrably closed before it. Whether they are opened in our time to the saving of our world depends on the joint efforts of all Christians.

CHAPTER VI

Christian Faith and Ethical Action

A GENERATION ago Walter Rauschenbusch wrote his *Theology for the Social Gospel* to undergird the emerging social gospel movement in the churches. Several notable facts have given this book lasting value: (1) the author's discernment that a theology was needed which would be both more inclusive and more incisive than the familiar and easily mouthed "fatherhood of God and brotherhood of man," (2) the range and depth with which the author actually succeeded in setting forth such a theology in reference to his particular theme, and (3) the centrality of the Kingdom of God, in terms of which the rest of the system was bound together. The book still deserves to be read. Certain emphases need to be added to meet the emergence of a historical situation which, with all the tragic facts of the First World War, Rauschenbusch could not prevision; and if he were writing now, what he says of both the Kingdom of God and the kingdom of evil might be put in a different setting. Yet in its general theological structure the book has so much truth and so little error that it deservedly stands as a landmark in American theology.

What is greatly needed now is a fresh approach—either a modified form of Rauschenbusch's or some other if a truer can be found—which can be preached, discussed in lay groups, read and understood by laymen, brought to bear by laymen on political and economic action. Some very commendable writing on Christian ethics has been done in recent years. Most of it, however, has been pitched at a level to be read by seminary professors and ministers, and I am forced regretfully to believe that relatively little of it has reached the eye or the mind of the rank-and-file layman who must do the living that is written about. Here is a gulf we have hardly more than begun to span. Yet in a world as secularized as ours is, both without and within the Church, there is not much likelihood that social action will be vitally and intelligently Christian unless it roots in a vital and true theology.

This is not, of course, to imply that even the best of theology would cure all our social ills and make the world over. It will take a great deal of love in action, joined with technical wisdom, to do this. Love in action calls for the dynamic, propulsive power of the Christian evangel, and we shall need to acquire all possible skills from the natural and social sciences if we are not to act blunderingly. Nevertheless, with a poor theology or in the absence of any we shall make worse mistakes, for in what has to be done goals will be distorted and we shall not see clearly enough our own relations to the work of God. The most important factor in any situation is what God requires of us and what God offers in the way of power to see it through.

In what follows no attempt will be made to cover the whole gamut of theology as it bears on Christian ethical decision. The things most commonly affirmed by those of social conscience are in general true and need not here be labored. That God is our Father and all men are brothers; that love is the great commandment; that men are sinners but also of supreme worth and dignity in God's sight; that we are knit together, body and soul, in such fashion that both the bodies and souls of men must be served and saved; that the individual cannot fulfill his God-given destiny apart from society—these basic foundations of a Christian social ethic will be assumed. This is not to say that these notes are already fully accepted. They are far from being accepted in practice and must continue to be preached. But it may be more fruitful here to center attention on other points at which errors or inadequacies in theology inhibit fruitful social action.

Let us therefore look rapidly at three great doctrines of the Christian faith—creation, judgment, and redemption. With the last I shall link the closely related concept of the Kingdom of God.

Creation. The most elemental meeting place of the

Christian with the secular mind is at the point of the doctrine of creation. The world is here and we are in it—this is an indisputable fact among many uncertainties. It is, furthermore, in its natural aspects an extremely intricate and law-abiding world, hardly to be conceived of as the product of accident or chance. Increasing scientific knowledge, far from disproving the existence of God, has seemed to many to give clear evidence that a Supreme Intelligence is the source of our world. The vogue of Lecomte du Noüy's *Human Destiny* is at least partly to be accounted for by the fact that it gives scientific corroboration to what many readers already believed, or wanted to believe. In any case the fact that the existence of the universe is not self-explanatory seems obvious enough so that, except where mechanistic or naturalistic philosophies have inculcated a contrary view, assent is usually readily given to the view that a Supreme Power has made the world.

This, however, is still a long way from the Christian doctrine of creation. The *Ladies' Home Journal* poll reports that while 95 per cent of the people questioned said they believed in God, only 26 per cent in subsequent answers seemed to indicate that they think of God as being in any way intimately related to their own lives. To the others God is "Creator" or "Supreme Power" or vaguely "spirit." To hosts of people creation is essentially a deistic process—something that took place a long time ago when the world was set in operation, but which has little if anything to do with us now.

The Christian doctrine of creation requires interpretation and application at several vital points. The essential goodness of creation, the union in the Creator of holiness and majesty with personal concern, man's delegated responsibility and stewardship, and the unfinished character of creation are all aspects of the doctrine which have great social importance.

Running like a great refrain through the poem of creation in the first chapter of Genesis are the words, "And God saw that it was good." This is an insight we ought never to lose. In the midst of personal tragedy, global disaster, or the threat of man's total destruction we need to remember that this is God's world, and a good world. Not even an approximate solution of the problem of evil, and in particular natural evil, is possible without this confidence. In the conviction that "This is my Father's world," and

> That though the wrong seems oft so strong,
> God is the Ruler yet,

anything can be endured and an incentive found to do what one can to help right the wrong. Without such a confidence life loses much of its meaning, hope turns to despair, and it is easy to believe that the world is not the work of God the Creator at all, but simply "the trampling march of unconscious power." That this has so widely happened in our day is at least part of the reason for current cynicism and nervelessness in the effort to secure peace and justice in human relations.

The Christian doctrine of creation implies also that the High and Holy One, whose ways are not our ways and whose thoughts are not our thoughts, is also the God who is intimately near. Both the majestic holiness and transcendence of God and his immanence need to be stressed to give the right incentives to Christian ethics. Liberalism has sometimes so overemphasized the immanence of God that it has skirted close to pantheism or humanism, and has lost the sense of great divine imperatives from the God who "hath made us, and not we ourselves." This is probably the major source of its relatively slight ethical influence in spite of its continuous moral injunctions. However, the other extreme of putting God so far off that he has little if any connection with men through the natural order is even more destructive to ethical action. We do need "Christian Marshall Plans" both in the political order and in the Church; and if Christians cannot feel that God is present in personal loving concern both in the natural order and in the persons he has created, it is but a step to the conclusion that no God that matters exists anywhere.

To say that God cares about his whole creation is not to say that he cares about the physical or the subhuman biological world in just the same way that he does for persons. In all probability for him as for us the physical order is an instrumental and not an intrinsic good, and life apart from the human spirit is less meaningful and precious. Yet to assume that in everything but man there is a vast indifference is to open the door to the suspicion that it is only a fragment, and not the whole, of the world that is God's world. In the literature outside the Bible I know of nothing which more vividly and in a spiritual sense more accurately portrays the intimate regard of God for his whole creation than James Weldon Johnson's sermon on creation in *God's Trombones.* Obviously anthropomorphic and in need of translation for rational purposes into other language, it has in it the majestic overtones and delicate resonance of a divine concern for all that is. Man needs to love the world because it is God's world before he can cease to be enticed by it in self-love, and without something of a shared concern for the earth and all its resources we are not likely to work with God in a shared enterprise to use them for human good.

This brings us to a third aspect of the doctrine of creation, man's delegated responsibility and stewardship. The biblical account of creation leaves no doubt about the fact that man's lordship over the earth is a gift of God in trust, not a natural right and not something man has earned. A fuller recognition of this fact would challenge current assumptions from two directions. In the first place, we should have less of self-righteous pride in our technological achievements, and the implicit humanism of a secular society which finds both its chief goals and chief supports in man's mastery of nature might be somewhat sobered. Our economic life is at present largely organized on a "little Jack Horner" basis, and both the pulling of plums from the common pie and the consequent exclamations of individual pride are contrary to the Christian understanding of man's relation to the Source of his being. And, second, a conception of stewardship which has often been limited to tithing might be broadened to incorporate a sense of responsibility for the more socially productive use of what has been entrusted to men. The waste or misuse of natural resources—whether in soil erosion, exploitation of oil or gas or steam or electric power for private gain, or the use of atomic energy for human destruction—has not yet come to be viewed by many Christians as a sin against God. If the question, "Will a man rob God?" were put searchingly enough, a conscience might eventually be aroused as to whether this has not some connection with robbing one's fellow men through private appropriation of what God in the act of creation has intended for all.

A fourth major deduction from a Christian doctrine of creation is that creation is still going on, and in this process man has a place as God's servant. This is less obvious than the other points noted, for the biblical story of creation is in the past tense and reads as if the process ended with the creation of man. However, if the biblical doctrine of God as the Lord of history is put in conjunction with creation, it becomes abundantly clear both in the Old Testament and in the New that "My Father worketh even until now," and expects men to work with him. Glancing into a small and by no means complete concordance to locate this reference, I was surprised to find nearly five hundred passages referring to work, these being about equally divided between God's work and man's work. The Bible is an extremely activistic book. It is a distortion of the biblical view to suppose that the eternity of creation implies a timelessness in which God, as a disinterested spectator, views the whole from the standpoint of an "eternal now." It is equally a distortion to regard God as simply *primus inter pares* in the co-working of God and man. Nevertheless, it is deeply imbedded in the biblical view that God's work is not done yet, that it will not be until the Kingdom is consummated, and that in the fashioning of the world nearer to the purposes of God man as God's servant has an indispensable part to play.

Indeed, any other view is both so static and so totalitarian that, regardless of professed doctrine, our moral intuitions recoil. The vogue of the unfortunate phrase "building the Kingdom of God" has lain in the emphasis it gives to the fact that man, together with God, has still some creative work to do. Though the phrase had better be abandoned for something less open to the charge of self-righteousness, the meaning it conveys of responsible creativity is a note which can be surrendered only at great loss. The parable of the sower gives a better simile, for while men must sow the seed, amid risks that are shared by God and man, it is God who gives the fruitage. The more such ongoing, divine-human creativity is made to seem relevant to political and social action, the more enthusiasm ("God within us") and hence effective accomplishment can be hoped for. Without it hope and confidence of change bog down, motives turn inward and go stale, and to preserve the *status quo* appears the most we can expect.

Judgment. At the point of doctrine of divine judgment the modern mind finds both easy corroboration and an almost insurmountable stumbling block. The tragic events of the past generation are so directly traceable to human sin—particularly in the forms of acquisitiveness, national pride and arrogance, vindictiveness, cruelty, narrowness of outlook, and collective selfishness—that many sermons have been preached to demonstrate the existence of a moral order in the universe. On this foundation much has been said that is right and true regarding the doing of "the things which belong unto peace." This approach ought not to be disparaged; in fact it ought to be made oftener than it is. Yet it may be doubted whether in most of such sermons the full depths of the biblical doctrine of divine judgment are probed.

If the biblical concept of judgment is viewed as a

whole, it implies neither an automatically working moral order nor a God of wrath as this term is commonly understood. Judgment implies condemnation—a God of sternness, even severity, who cannot be complacent before sin. It means dynamic opposition to injustice and evil, terrible in the power of righteous indignation joined with righteous love. But at its center is a loving God "whose mercy endureth forever," and who because he desires righteousness in his erring children works both in the lives of individuals and the currents of history to win men to obedience. Punishment is not God's chosen way; it is his instrument only when men in stubborn self-will refuse either to cease their sinning or repent. The message of doom which resounds through the words of the prophets is never God's last word, and both the promise and the coming of the Deliverer lose much of their meaning unless they are seen as the positive side of the word of judgment.

If this is true, it is apparent that some serious mistakes are commonly made in Christian thinking about judgment. The first is an essentially deistic assumption that the moral order works automatically, and therefore whoever breaks the laws of God is broken upon them. This corresponds to the assumption regarding physical nature that natural law has been inaugurated by God but operates without specific divine intervention in particular events. In both instances there is an important half-truth which, taken by itself, becomes untruth.

There are apparently great continuing processes, moral as well as physical, through which God acts within his world; but this is not to say that he acts in indifference to the individuals concerned. What is left out of a deistic view of judgment is a sense of divine intimacy and concern—the living God who is grieved not only at the sin of mankind but at *our own* sins and who seeks in love to win us to obedience. Because this preaching of an automatic moral order so often sounds impersonal, it may be questioned whether it elicits as much repentance and personal passion for righteousness as did the older preaching of "sinners in the hands of an angry God."

But if liberalism has erred in the direction of making judgment too impersonal, the orthodoxies, old and new, have made it too wrathful. The term "God of wrath" has again come back into popular theological parlance, and with dubious gain. In spite of efforts to reinterpret it and remove some of the more obviously anthropomorphic connotations of spite and petty jealousy, both the natural connotation of the term and much of its context in current usage still sound pretty wrathful.

This is a matter of central importance from the standpoint of both biblical interpretation and Christian ethics. That numerous references to the wrath of God appear in both the Old and New Testaments cannot be disputed. Nevertheless, it may still be questioned whether a God of wrath can be fitted in with Jesus' understanding of the nature of God. God's displeasure—or better, his sorrow—at man's sin is bedrock for Christian belief; his anger at sinners is contrary to every basic note in the New Testament. Furthermore, "righteous indignation" is safe only with God. The moment the door is opened to a view of judgment which makes God wrathful in the sense of vindictive toward any of his sinful human children, at that moment we begin to find alibis for our own vindictive passions. Under cover of such a doctrine of divine justice man's own sense of justice loses the quality of mercy, and the bars are down to approve obliteration bombing or any other atrocity which modern warfare seems to call for.

Two illustrations may be in order at this point. It ought not to be said that every supporter of a "just" war does so on the basis of belief in a God of wrath. Yet there is more than a little connection between what we think of the judgment of God and the way we approve our own acts as instruments of that judgment. The modern mind has not really made a great deal of progress since ancient Israel in the matter of viewing the nation's enemies as God's enemies. Our bombs, battleships, bacteriological laboratories, and potentially our "satellite vehicle platforms" take on a more terrible and ominous sanctity when viewed, not simply as supposed instruments of security, but as instruments for the infliction of divine judgment upon those who contemn God's holy name and flout his law. It would appear that large portions of the Christian world have yet to discover the word of the New Testament: "Vengeance is mine; I will repay, saith the Lord. Therefore if thine enemy hunger, feed him. . . . Be not overcome of evil, but overcome evil with good."

A closely related example of the practical bearing of the problem is found in the fact that the most serious menace to the peace of the world is now to be found in attitudes of mutual recrimination between communists and those who in general consider themselves Christians. To hate—or at least to condemn—communism is one thing; to hate communists is another. God must draw the distinction, but we seldom do. Communism is not wholly evil, and in its concern for race equality and the alleviation of poverty for the underprivileged it is what the late Archbishop Temple called it in contrast with Nazi paganism, "a Christian heresy." Yet as far as we can read the mind of God in Christ, the all-righteous and all-loving God must judge many of its tenets and doings evil and at the same time seek in love the redemption of its adherents. If Christians in any considerable numbers were to try to make this their policy, the security as well as the justice of the world could be greatly enhanced.

To move to a different angle of the doctrine of divine judgment, a third major error—or perhaps, confusion—about it is based less on a wrong theology than on the lack of a right one. This appears in the inability of most of our laymen to find any credible answer to the problem, "Why do the righteous suffer while sinners prosper?" It is not difficult to find a correlation between a nation's collapse and the undermining of its foundations by sin and shallowness; history past and present gives numerous illustrations. Indeed, after a war the correlation is apt by the victors to be too closely drawn, overlooking factors other than their superior righteousness which determined the outcome. But such correspondence between goodness and success as can be seen in the rise and fall of nations seems not to have its counterpart in individual experience. Nothing is clearer than that goodness gives no immunity from pain, and on the whole a good many sinners seem to get along pretty well. Of course "honesty is the best policy," and "crime does not pay." But one is neither dishonest nor a criminal, and if one needs to take a few chances with shady practices to get ahead in business or romance or war, why be inhibited?

What this eventuates in is that even where the reality of sin and divine judgment are admitted, it often happens that no very pointed personal application is made by the individual to himself. Sin and judgment, conceived as general categories applicable to somebody else, do not strike home with the potency of "Thou art the man!" It is quite possible to believe that everybody needs to repent—and certainly that one's obstreperous neighbor does—without any searching sense of personal contrition. This is particularly true regarding large-scale social sins like race prejudice, and perhaps throws light on why so many good social gospel sermons seem to produce so little fruit.

Nor can the issue be met any longer simply by pointing to deferred penalties for sin. In our society—at least in the Protestant portion of it—there has been a major fading out of any individual fear of divine judgment, either here or hereafter. This may mark some progress from the day when the fear of hell was a dominant motive to Christian ethical action. But if nothing is put in its place, what we have is not gain but loss. The lack of any eschatological undergirding for Christian action is certainly a mark of our secularization and is probably also one of its dominant causes. In any case it goes along with the loss of a vital sense of sin, and without a sense of sin moral exhortations fall largely upon deaf ears.

I do not believe that the cure for this situation lies in the reinstatement of a fire-and-brimstone hell, or essentially in an appeal to motives of fear. However, there is no way out except through a better understanding of both judgment and redemption. We turn, therefore, to look at what redemption means in the context of our society.

Redemption and the Kingdom. The Christian doctrine of redemption, like the closely related concept of the Kingdom of God, needs to be viewed in several polar relations, in which the omission of either aspect of a fundamental duality introduces distortion. The Kingdom of God is the righteous and triumphant rule of God over a redeemed society—thus far Christians generally go in agreement. But how that rule is to come about, or when, or where, and what the relation is between a society of the redeemed and the redemption of society as a whole are matters about which widely diverse judgments are held. Is the coming of the Kingdom through the coming into being of such a redeemed society the work of man or the gift of God? Is it in some measure a present attainment, or is it a future hope? Is it to be consummated in this world or the next? Is it to be found only in the fellowship of redeemed Christians, or has it a wider context in the elimination of social evil and the creation of conditions of the good life for all men? What is the relation of Jesus Christ to it? Did he bring the Kingdom with him in his own historical incarnation? Does it come as men receive him today? Will he usher it in when he returns in glory? The mere listing of such questions uncovers a nest of problems, and anyone who has ever attended an ecumenical conference has seen them emerging in full force to thwart agreement and make it difficult to speak with a united voice on what lies at the heart of our faith and message.

It is obviously a mistake to blur distinctions and try to hold all of these views at once as equally true. Nevertheless, the fact that most of them have been held for centuries and defended on scriptural grounds by men who were not only sincere but intelligent Christians, should give us pause before rejecting them *in toto.* The one most widely prevalent in America—so widely held as to be regarded by many as *the* doctrine of the Kingdom—is the one with the shortest tradition behind it and the least explicit biblical foundation. Nevertheless, this social gospel Kingdom need not be dismissed if it emphasizes fundamental elements implicit, even though not expressly stated, in the teaching of Jesus.

The reason the Church has held all these views in rich profusion is not mainly to be found in the vagaries of the human mind. The deeper reason is that in a vital unity—not an abstract system but a living insight into man's relation to God—Jesus seems to have held them. What we have to do is to get at these profoundly true though apparently contradictory insights of Jesus and put them together in such systematic unity as we can without forcing their meaning.

Let us take a brief look at some of the questions above —not certainly with any idea of answering them in full, but to see how any attempt at an answer that seeks to be guided by the mind of Christ must take into account these polar aspects.

The first question to be considered is, "Are we justified in linking redemption with the Kingdom? Can there be any redemption apart from the coming of the Kingdom? Is the Kingdom what 'salvation through Christ' means?" In the writings of Paul and throughout the history of Christian thought before the nineteenth century these concepts were largely kept in separate categories, and surprisingly little was said about the Kingdom. The primary notes in Christian redemption are man's need of repentance and the availability of mercy, forgiveness, and the new life through God's grace; and these have not been—indeed, are not now—the dominant notes in discussions of the Kingdom. Yet to separate redemption from the Kingdom is an artificial wrenching which distorts the message of Jesus. The conditions of membership in the Kingdom are faith and love, expressed in repentance, confident trust, purity of heart, humility, mercy, forgiveness, loving service to God and neighbor. I am unable to discover that Jesus made any separation between what is now called individual and social salvation, or between entrance into the Kingdom and entrance into new life through the power and grace of God.

Any such separation not only is untrue to the primary message of Jesus, but has disastrous social consequences. Perhaps the major tragedy of Christian history is the fact that personal salvation has so largely been conceived apart from its social context, and as a consequence too little attention has been given either to the social factors which beget sin or to the social fruits of the redeemed life. I have not seen this put more forthrightly than by the late Nicholas Berdyaev in his article in the first issue of *The Ecumenical Review*:

Can we go on interpreting Christianity as solely the religion of *personal* salvation in the eternal life—which means transferring selfishness to the world beyond? Such an interpretation is the main source of reactionary motives in Christianity. A religion of merely *personal* salvation is an essential contradiction to the good news of the coming of God's Kingdom. That Kingdom means not only a personal but a social and a cosmic transfiguration.[1]

If one looks around today at the movements within Christianity which are most reactionary, it is apparent that what Berdyaev says is true, and emphasis on personal salvation outside the context of the Kingdom runs into a form of selfishness which is the antithesis of anything that Jesus taught. If there is any redemption at all, it must be within a social framework, though this leaves still open the question of the kind of society the Kingdom connotes.

The crux of all the problems in this field—indeed, the central problem confronting the Church—is the nature of the society that constitutes, or will constitute, the Kingdom of God. Is the Kingdom composed only of committed followers of Jesus Christ, in such a sense that "the saved" here will be saved hereafter, destined to dwell with God in the bliss and glory of an eternal fellowship? Or does the Kingdom mean such a transformation of earthly society that all men—whether

[1] "The Unity of Christendom in the Strife Between East and West," in the *Ecumenical Review,* I, 1 (Autumn, 1948), p. 15.

saints or not, and perhaps whether Christians or not—will be treated as persons of intrinsic dignity, and will be able without man-made barriers to enjoy "the abundant life" and dwell together in peace, justice, and good will? There is much to commend either view, but it is not easy to get these two views together. To the defenders of either, the adherents to the other are apt to appear reactionary, blasphemous, or in any case deluded.

As in most matters, the extremists in either camp are wrong. As we have just noted, any exclusive emphasis on personal salvation, whether for this life or the next, runs into a form of selfishness which is the antithesis of the teaching and spirit of Jesus. Nor is this remedied when the implicit egotism of such a view becomes the "we-gotism" of assuming that Christians alone—perhaps only our brand of Christians—are children of God having favor in God's sight. But it is equally a departure from authentic Christianity to interpret "the abundant life" as economic abundance, or cultural achievement, or even the establishment of the conditions of a free and democratic society. Christians have lived in the Kingdom of God in the absence of all these conditions, and if necessary will presumably continue to do so.

To get these two views together certain great admissions and affirmations must be made. The first is that there is a kind of salvation, and hence some measure of the coming of the Kingdom, outside of personally committed Christian experience and outside of Christendom. God has "left not himself without witness" among any people. This point, so sharply debated at the Madras Conference, needs to be affirmed to prevent Christian pharisaism. As Paul Tillich has reminded us, besides the "manifest church" there is a "latent church" in labor movements, in efforts for international understanding and racial equality, even in some measure within communism. If this is true, it means that membership in the Kingdom cannot be equated with membership in the visible Christian Church.

Yet this admission, though necessary, is at the same time exceedingly dangerous. It can safely be made only by those who stand squarely within the Church and the convictions of Christian faith, not by those outside or on the margin. Made by any except convinced Christians, the assertion that God has channels for the establishment of his Kingdom outside the witness committed by Christ to the Church is likely to run into alibis for personal indifference and a kind of easy tolerance in which the drastic demands and saving power of the gospel are lost. This has so largely happened that the emphasis on a transcendent and eschatological Kingdom of the redeemed in Christ needed to reappear. Yet this too needs correction by a closer linkage of a doctrine of *full* salvation through Christ alone with one that leaves an open end for God and man to work together through many channels for the creation of a universal community of love.

Is the Kingdom to come through man's achievement or God's act? The history of Christian thought for centuries has swung between these Pelagian and Augustinian, these Arminian and Calvinist poles. But if we consult the New Testament, nothing is clearer than that God brings in the Kingdom when man meets the conditions of obedience and faith which God imposes. "By grace are ye saved through faith" and "Work out your own salvation with fear and trembling" are equally authentic Christian notes. Where these notes have been held together, Christianity is virile. Where they have been separated, it becomes on the one hand socially reactionary and on the other religiously shallow. Nothing is much more needed in our time than to get them back into the undivided unity where Jesus and Paul had them.

Is the Kingdom here, or is it coming? I see no reason to doubt that when Jesus said, "The kingdom of God is in the midst of you," [2] he meant to stress its present attainability. Anyone who has participated in a great fellowship such as a world conference of Christians can scarcely doubt that, in spite of much human frailty and defense of vested ecclesiastical, theological, cultural, and personal interest, the Kingdom is already in some

[2] Luke 17:21 (R.S.V.).

measure present. Yet it would be arrant utopianism to suppose that in any group it is fully present, or that in any proposal for a new Church or a new society we have a panacea for ushering it in. Neither democracy, nor capitalism, nor communism, nor the United Nations, nor the ecumenical church is a straight highway to the Kingdom; yet presumably in each we have some fore-gleams of its reality.

Will the Kingdom ever fully be consummated on earth? Here extremes meet, for both utopian liberals trusting in evolutionary social processes and despairing premillennialists trusting in catastrophic divine intervention believe that it will be. The truth lies presumably in neither view but in the more restrained judgment that as long as human life lasts upon earth we shall still need to be praying, "Thy kingdom come. Thy will be done on earth." Such tentativeness is required by any serious reckoning with the pervasiveness of human sin. It is essential also to the Christian moral enterprise if we are to continue to act soberly but in hope, "perplexed but not unto despair," in obedience to the will of God and in the quest, not for a perfect, but for a better world.

We noted in a previous chapter the need of more positive preaching of the Christian view of death and immortality. The same holds true in the social sense. No adequate view of redemption or the Kingdom is possible without an eschatological note. Both the premillennialist and the exclusively social gospel Kingdoms are unsatisfactory because they are too earth-centered. Any view that is to be both true and dynamic—dynamic with the power of truth—must have in it the resonance of faith in God's triumph beyond the frustrations and proximate successes of the earthly scene. Regarding the form God's triumph will take "we see in a mirror dimly," but some assurances we have regarding membership in the eternal society: the continuance of personal existence, a fellowship of free spirits, moral endeavor in fuller obedience, growth in the things of God, closer companionship with Christ, the glory of God's nearer presence, the preservation by him of all that is truly worthful. Regarding these elements in the Christian hope we ought not to be too dogmatic, but neither ought they to be blurred over and passed by as utter mysteries.

In the confidence that for time and eternity our destinies are in God's hands we can labor with God for the advancement of his Kingdom, "rejoicing in hope; patient in tribulation; continuing instant in prayer." Without this confidence, held and propagated with greater earnestness and understanding by laymen and clergy alike, the time may not be far away when

> Our little systems have their day;
> They have their day and cease to be,

will become realized eschatology, and God's eternal Kingdom will alone be left.